INTRO

HISTORY, JESUS AND THE GOSPELS

History is important for Christianity. Why? Because the Christian faith is not primarily a bunch of ideas about the world, or a philosophy of life, but a claim about what happened in the past to a real man called Jesus. Christians believe that the world is different because of who Jesus *really* was, and because of the things he *really* did, and because of what *really* happened to him after he died. It's only because of what it says about *history* that Christianity has anything to say about life today.

You don't have to be a rocket scientist to understand that the truth about the events of Jesus' life matter. If, on the one hand, it turns out that Jesus didn't heal people and rise from the dead, then there's no point in anyone being a Christian. On the other hand, if Jesus really did the things Christians believe he did, then it matters for everyone. If Jesus rose from the dead then he's not just someone who would be interesting to meet at parties—in light of what he claimed about himself it would mean he's the ruler of the world.

The truth about Jesus matters, and so history matters—to Christians, and to everyone else as well. So the big question is: *how do we know*? How do we know what's true about Jesus? This brings us to the topic of this booklet: the Gospels.

The Gospels are the four stories of Jesus' life you can find at the beginning of the New Testament section of the Bible. They're titled Matthew, Mark, Luke and John. In most Bibles, the Gospels have been grouped together and printed nicely with footnotes and headings.

This is all very helpful, but it can make us forget that these are historical documents. They were written a very long time ago in a very different culture. They weren't originally printed in English with gold edging and footnotes!

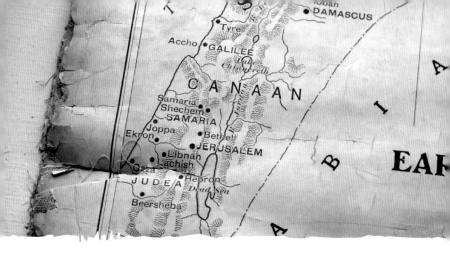

The Gospels are our main source of information about the real, historical Jesus. For about the last 2000 years, Christians have believed that the Gospels are reliable history. That is, they tell us the truth about who Jesus was and what he did. But is this opinion right? How do we know they weren't just made up? Can we really trust what the Gospels say about Jesus?

The rest of this booklet is about the many good reasons to answer 'yes' to that last question. There are three main sections: Part 1 ('Where did the Gospels come from?') looks at what we know about the authors of the Gospels and how their works have come down to us; Part 2 ('What are the Gospels?') seeks to avoid misunderstanding and misuse of the Gospels by getting a clear picture of what kind of documents they are; and Part 3 ('What evidence is there?') examines the evidence for the historical reliability of the Gospels from external sources and from within the Gospels themselves. The question of whether there are, as is sometimes claimed, other sources that tell us more about Jesus is discussed in an appendix at the end.

PART 1

WHERE DID THE GOSPELS COME FROM?

If you open any modern Bible, you'll see that the first four books of the New Testament are stories of Jesus' life titled Matthew, Mark, Luke and John—the four Gospels. Where did they come from? To answer this question there are three big issues we need to look at: how the Gospels were passed down to our time and into our Bibles; how they were originally written; and what we know about the people who wrote them. We'll start with the Gospels in our Bibles. How did they get to us?

How did they get to us?

When you look at the Gospels in a modern Bible, you're looking at a translation of a text originally written in ancient Greek. The Greek text that the translation comes from is constructed by comparing hundreds of ancient copies of the text with each other. These ancient copies date from anywhere between AD 120 and the Middle Ages. All of them are copies of earlier copies of the Gospels, which were also copied from earlier copies, which eventually go back to an original version, written in Greek. All of the original versions, however, have been lost.

Now, this all sounds a bit shaky doesn't it? Translations of lots of copies that aren't all the same, with no original to fix the mistakes—it doesn't exactly fill you with confidence! How do we know what the original documents were like?

As in many areas of life, first impressions are often deceptive. The vast majority of the differences between texts are of very little significance. They came about mostly through copying errors. The scribes who did the copying would make little errors, mistaking one word for another, or accidentally leaving out a word or a letter.

A good example of the kind of thing we're talking about is in Matthew chapter 6, verse 33. Jesus says, "seek first the kingdom of God and his righteousness, and all these things will be added to you". However, a number of early manuscripts have this passage without the words "of God". We can't be certain what the original text was here, but it makes no difference to the meaning of the passage. It's very clear that Jesus was talking about God's kingdom because it's the only kingdom he ever talked about. Most of the differences between versions of the Gospels are like this—they're pretty small and they don't make any real difference to what the text means.

However, there are a couple of points where the differences are more significant. The first is in Mark's Gospel. Our sources disagree over how Mark's Gospel originally ended. Most of the manuscripts have a long ending (chapter 16, verses 9-20), but the oldest don't, and some even have a mark in the margin to show that this section is a problem. So some scholars think that the original ending of the Gospel was lost. (In those days, books were written on scrolls, and the beginning and end of a scroll were the bits most easily damaged.) Others, however, think Mark just ends suddenly at chapter 16, verse 8. Now, unless archaeologists dig up some new copies of Mark, we're probably never going to be sure what the real ending was.

Does it matter? Well, not really. Although it would be interesting to know the answer to this puzzle, the ending wouldn't change much of what we know about Jesus. We have records of what happened in the days after Jesus was buried in three other Gospels, so even if the ending of Mark is lost, it's not very important.

The other major place where there's a question about the original version is an interesting story in John's Gospel (John chapter 7, verse 53 to chapter 8, verse 11). The difficult thing is that the oldest manuscripts don't have this story. So most scholars think it wasn't originally in John's Gospel. Does it matter? Again, not very much. We can't treat this story like it was definitely part of the first version of John's Gospel, but it may still give us good information about the historical Jesus.

Both of these examples are clearly noted in any modern Bible and they really are the most significant problems with the text. We actually have few difficulties in working out what the original Gospels said.

A little comparison with another ancient source is helpful here. One very important ancient work is *The Jewish War*, by a first-century Jewish historian named Josephus. There are only nine remaining complete manuscripts of *The Jewish War* in existence, and the oldest of these is a fifth-century Latin translation. Yet scholars are confident that the text of *The Jewish War* is pretty clear, even though there aren't that many copies and there is around a 400-year gap between the original and our oldest copy. By contrast, there are literally thousands of copies of the Gospels (or parts of the Gospels), some of which date from only 50 years or so after the originals. The truth is that we have a more reliable text of the Gospels than almost any other ancient work.

But where did these *original* Gospels come from? How did Matthew, Mark, Luke and John come to be written? This is the next crucial question.

How did they get written?

We don't know exactly when the Gospels were written, but we've got a pretty good idea. For starters, it's clear that they were all written by the end of the first century AD. After this, people start quoting them—a sure sign they'd been around for a while. What's more, a piece of John's Gospel has been found that dates from the early second century (it has the exciting name of 'Rylands Papyrus 457'). Most scholars date Mark between AD 60 and 70, Matthew and Luke around ten years after Mark, and John by around AD 90. Others think that all these dates are too late and that the Gospels were actually written a fair bit earlier. Jesus was executed around AD 33,[1] so this means there were roughly 30 years between his death and the earliest books about him. 30 years! Sounds like a long time. Can we be confident that the things Jesus said and did weren't changed or forgotten by the time the Gospels were written?

Well, it all depends on how this information was passed down. If information about Jesus passed through 30 years of careless memory before it got to the Gospels, we may as well throw them out as nonsense. But thankfully, that's not what happened. The Gospels were produced in a world where writing wasn't the standard form of communication. In many countries today we take it for granted that most people can read and write, but it wasn't like that in the first century. Possibly only 10-15% of people could read and write at this time, so writing a book wasn't the best way to communicate. Instead, pieces of information or stories were often passed on orally—that is, by hearing them and repeating them aloud; and the evidence shows that cultures that rely on these forms of communication can remember things very accurately indeed.

What's more, there are good reasons to think Jesus' teaching would have been especially well remembered. Jesus' disciples were with him for around three years. They would have heard him teach many times as he adapted his stories and messages to suit each different audience, so they probably had more than one chance to remember things. Also, a lot of Jesus' teaching was naturally memorable. This is why lots of people know some of Jesus' sayings, such as "Do unto others as you would have them do unto you", and "You are the salt of the earth". Lots of the things Jesus said are like this—you only have to hear them once and they stick with you. But even more significantly, Jesus' followers believed that he was the Messiah, the Son of God. It would be very odd if they believed this but didn't make an effort to remember the things he said. As Peter said to Jesus: "You have the words of eternal life" (John chapter 6, verse 68). These are not words he'd want to forget in a hurry!

What's also very important is that some of Jesus' disciples remained alive until the Gospels were produced. These disciples almost certainly played a significant role in making sure the oral traditions about Jesus remained accurate. Those who had been eyewitnesses of Jesus from the beginning of his public life became leaders in the early church and would have functioned as guardians of the tradition, making sure that Jesus' words and deeds were remembered rightly. That is, it wasn't like a 30-year game of 'Chinese Whispers'![2] The living eyewitnesses safeguarded the reliability of the oral traditions about Jesus.[3]

In fact, it was probably partly the dying out of this group of people that prompted the Gospels to be written—the tradition had to be preserved beyond the lifetime of the eyewitnesses, and so the Gospels were produced as the record of their testimony. It appears that Mark's

Gospel—very likely the record of Peter's teaching about Jesus—was written first, because it looks like Matthew and Luke based what they were writing on Mark's version (to which they added other material). Of course, we don't know exactly how it all happened—lots of things remain a mystery—but there's every reason to think that the Gospels accurately record what the real Jesus said and did, because the words and deeds of Jesus were very carefully remembered.

But who wrote them down, and what do we know about these authors? Can they be trusted to have done a good job?

What do we know about the authors?

As far back as we can go, the Gospels have had the names they've got in our Bibles: Matthew, Mark, Luke and John. Since very early on, Christians have thought these meant the apostle Matthew, Mark (a companion of Peter), Luke (a travelling companion of the apostle Paul), and either the apostle John or another disciple of Jesus named John. Now, this may very well be right, but the truth is that we can't be one hundred percent certain about who wrote the Gospels. However, being able to name the authors is not the most important thing. What's a lot more interesting is what we can discover about the goals, intentions and beliefs of these authors. We can get a good picture of what they thought they were doing in writing their stories about Jesus. Luke's Gospel, for example, begins with these words:

> Since many have undertaken to set down an orderly account of the events that have been fulfilled among us, just as they were handed on to us by those who from the beginning were eyewitnesses and servants of the word, I too decided, after investigating everything carefully from the very first, to write an orderly account for you, most excellent Theophilus, so that you may know the truth concerning the things about which you have been instructed. (Luke chapter 1, verses 1-4, NRSV)

Luke claims to tell the truth about the events of Jesus' life. He's up-front about the fact that he has used sources, and says his information comes

THE GOSPEL ACCORDING TO SAINT MATTHEW

CHAPTER 1

from people who were there from the beginning—the 'eyewitnesses' we mentioned earlier.

At the end of John's Gospel there's a similar kind of statement. Referring to one of Jesus' closest companions, it says:

> This is the disciple who is bearing witness about these things, and who has written these things, and we know that his testimony is true. (John chapter 21, verse 24)

The one who wrote the things in John's Gospel was someone who knew Jesus personally, and who could be trusted to tell the truth. The conclusion is clear: the authors of the Gospels believed they were writing accurate history. They emphasized the fact that they had good information from eyewitnesses, because it mattered to the Gospel writers that they were telling the truth about Jesus.

This fact—that the Gospel writers wanted to be truthful—shouldn't be a surprise. Everything we know about the early Christians should lead us to expect this. To begin with, not lying was an important part of the Christian teaching. The apostle Paul, in letters to early Christian churches, wrote, "Do not lie to one another ..." (Colossians chapter 3, verse 9), and "Therefore, having put away falsehood, let each one of you speak the truth with his neighbor" (Ephesians chapter 4, verse 25). And the early Christians described their faith as "the truth" (e.g. 1 Timothy chapter 2, verse 4; chapter 3, verse 15; 1 Peter chapter 1, verse 22). It would be pretty hypocritical, to put it mildly, if people who said these kinds of things didn't worry about whether they were writing accurately or not. They were people who believed in telling the truth; they weren't about to make up fairytales and call them history.

Writing truthfully also mattered to the authors of the Gospels because of their religious background. Along with all the other people who wrote the books in the New Testament, the Gospel writers came from a Jewish background. Their Bible was what we now call the Old Testament and they wrote the Gospels partly to show how the story of the Old Testament had come to its climax with Jesus. What difference does this make? Well, the Jewish background of the Gospel writers meant that they cared a lot about history. When you read the Old Testament, you find that it's all about the history of Israel. God is the God who rescues Israel from Egypt, brings them through the desert and gives them the Promised Land.

This Jewish God works within history. He's not some far-away God who just tells people how to live and then doesn't get involved in life. He gets his hands dirty and makes himself known in the real world. This was the God the Gospel writers believed in and this was the God they thought had acted in Jesus. So it mattered a lot to them that they were talking about things that had really happened. *God was a God who worked within history, and so history mattered to the Gospel writers.*

Conclusion

Well, what can we conclude from all this? The Gospels in our Bibles have come down to us from a long time ago. They have been copied and translated and copied and translated. Despite all this, we know that when we read them today, we're pretty much reading what the originals said. These originals were produced close to the time of Jesus' life and death, and were based on good information. Finally, everything we know about the authors of the Gospels gives us confidence that they can be trusted. They claimed to be writing solid history based on good evidence. They believed in telling the truth, and they believed that God was a God who acted within history. All this is a good first step; but we need to go further. If we want to work out whether we can trust the Gospels, then we need to get a better handle on what they actually are.

PART 2

WHAT ARE THE GOSPELS?

What are the Gospels? At first glance, this might seem like a silly question. We know what the Gospels are—they're histories of Jesus. This is true, but when you look at the Gospels it becomes clear that they're not *mere* history. They don't seem to be straight-up-and-down accounts of 'the facts' about Jesus. So we need to take a more detailed look at this question of what the Gospels actually are. We'll see, first, that the Gospels are carefully constructed stories that don't try to say everything, and second, that they're written from a particular point of view—that is, they're not 'neutral'.

Carefully constructed stories that don't try to say everything

When you read the Gospels, it becomes clear that they're different from each other. There are things in some Gospels that aren't in the others, and each of them 'sounds' slightly different from the others. For instance, Matthew, Mark and Luke all record Jesus telling a lot of parables (short stories designed to make a powerful point); but John's Gospel doesn't have any parables at all. And it looks like they have all left things out. Unlike modern biographies, which normally try to cover a person's whole life, the Gospels ignore most of Jesus' first 30 years. So it seems that, whatever the Gospels are, they weren't designed to tell us *everything* about Jesus. Does this mean that the Gospels don't qualify as history, or that we can't trust them?

It's important to realize that the people who wrote the Gospels were quite up-front about all this. John's Gospel ends with these words:

> Now there are also many other things that Jesus did. Were
> every one of them to be written, I suppose that the world itself
> could not contain the books that would be written. (John
> chapter 21, verse 25)

And just a little bit earlier it says this:

> Now Jesus did many other signs in the presence of the disciples,
> which are not written in this book … (John chapter 20, verse 30)

John didn't pretend to be telling the *whole* story, so to speak. He knew
he wasn't saying everything there was to say and he made sure his
readers were clear on that as well. We might have wanted him to pack in
everything he knew about Jesus, but that's not what he did.

Instead, John and the other Gospel writers thought carefully about
what they would include and what they would leave out,[4] constructing
their accounts of Jesus' life with great care and expertise. The Gospels
are cleverly written pieces of literature. So, for example, in the first
half of his Gospel, John has arranged various 'signs' or miracles done
by Jesus, to highlight different things about him. Things Jesus did are
placed next to things he said to bring out the point, such as when John
records Jesus saying, "I am the light of the world" (John chapter 8,
verses 12-30 and chapter 9, verse 5) and then describes him healing
a man who was born blind (John chapter 9).

Equally interestingly, Matthew's Gospel is written partly to show how
the story of the Old Testament came true in Jesus. It constantly draws
attention to the ways in which Jesus *fulfilled* things the Old Testament
said, inserting quotations to show that the whole story of Israel was
coming to its climax in Jesus (see, for example, Matthew chapter 1, verses
22-23; chapter 2, verses 1-6 and 14-18; chapter 12, verses 15-21).

Sometimes when we read the Gospels we can miss what intricate
pieces of writing they really are. However, when we look closely, it's
clear that John and Matthew didn't just whack things together in any
old way. Like painters creating beautiful artworks, they chose what
colours and textures to work with, and what to leave out.

Understanding this helps us to avoid some common traps.
Sometimes, it can look like the Gospels contradict each other when

in fact they're just not saying everything there is to say. A classic example of this is that Matthew records Jesus healing two blind men on the Jericho Road (Matthew chapter 20, verse 30), but Mark records him healing only one (Mark chapter 10, verse 46). At first glance, it looks like either Matthew or Mark has got it wrong. But actually, the accounts don't contradict each other. Mark may simply have wanted to call attention to one of the men in particular, and not felt the need to mention both. If Mark and Matthew had been witnesses in a courtroom responding to detailed questions and they'd been asked, "How many blind men did Jesus heal?", and they gave different answers, then we'd have a problem. But the Gospels are not detailed witness statements; they are different, carefully arranged accounts of the same incredible events. We shouldn't expect the Gospels to agree on every detail. The authors included some things and left other bits out because of the story they were telling, not because they didn't care about the truth.

So the Gospels are carefully constructed stories that don't say everything, and don't need to. This is the first thing we need to see if we want to make sure we use them correctly. Just as important is the second thing we need to look at: the Gospels are all written from a particular point of view.

Written from a point of view (they're not 'neutral')

The Gospels are quite up-front about the fact that they're coming from a particular perspective. Mark's Gospel begins with these words:

> The beginning of the gospel [or 'good news'] of Jesus Christ, the Son of God. (Mark chapter 1, verse 1)

Mark wants everyone who reads his story to be in no doubt about who he thinks Jesus is. He believes that Jesus is the Son of God and he makes it the first thing he says. John's Gospel has a similar kind of statement near the end of the book. It says:

> Now Jesus did many other signs in the presence of the
> disciples, which are not written in this book; but these are
> written so that you may believe that Jesus is the Christ, the Son
> of God, and that by believing you may have life in his name.
> (John chapter 20, verses 30-31)

John is open about why he's writing. He wants to convince people that Jesus is the Son of God. The Gospels were all written by people who believed that Jesus was the Son of God and that his life, death and resurrection were incredibly important. They don't try to hide this and pretend they're neutral; they fly their flag for everyone to see.

Some people might throw up their hands at this point and say, "Look, I don't care if they're open—they're biased! How can we trust them? How can we treat them as history?" There are two important things to say here.

First, neutral perspectives are actually pretty hard to find. The reality is that everyone has a point of view. Everyone comes from a certain perspective that colours the way they see the world. Whether they're talking to you about a football match or writing someone's biography, *people are coming from somewhere*. In fact, it's a good idea to be a bit careful about anyone who claims to be 'just telling the facts'. It should make us ask questions like, "Which facts?", and "Why these facts and not other facts?" Rather than pretending to be neutral, it's best if people are up-front about where they're coming from.

The Gospel writers don't try to pretend to be neutral and then sneak in their opinions while you're not looking. Their point of view is written down for everyone to see, and this should encourage us to think they're being honest.

Second, bias can be a helpful thing. Think for a moment about cricket. If you knew nothing at all about cricket, and you wanted to find out how it worked, what went on, and what made it a good game, then you could do a number of things:

1. You could go to a cricket rulebook. This would have the advantage of giving you 'the facts' very clearly. Yet, it's unlikely that this would inspire you to take up a bat and ball.

2. Alternatively, you could talk to someone who basically doesn't like cricket. This means the information you get won't be clouded by any positive feelings about the game. However, there are good reasons to question whether they will really give the game a fair go, or even know about the details of the game.

3. Finally, you could talk to someone who loves cricket—a cricket fan. Now, their opinion will obviously be biased and you'll have to be aware of that, but at least you'll get to know the game from the inside out. You'll get a sense of why people like it and what makes it interesting. The fact that you're talking to a fan won't mean you have to distrust everything they say. I might be the biggest cricket fan in the world, but that doesn't mean I'm lying if I say that when a batsman hits the ball over the boundary on the full, he scores six runs. That would just be silly. A fan will know the rules and the history of the game a whole lot better than someone who hates cricket.

It's sort of the same with the Gospels. When we read them, we have to be aware that they're coming from the perspective of 'a fan'. We need to remember that the authors of the Gospels believed Jesus was the Son of God and wrote their stories to tell people about him. But that doesn't mean we can't trust what they say. In fact, sometimes talking to a fan can be the best way to find out about something! And we also need to remember that the Gospel writers only became 'fans' in the first place because of the *historical* events they saw and words they heard spoken.

Conclusion

In Part 1 we saw that the Gospel writers were on about history and were interested in the truth about Jesus. However, the Gospels aren't *mere* history. They're not the 'bare facts', like a cricket rulebook. Instead, they're carefully constructed stories about Jesus that don't say everything and don't pretend to; they're written from a particular point of view—the point of view of someone who trusts in Jesus.

We've got to remember these things when we read the Gospels, otherwise we'll end up using them in the wrong way. Matthew, Mark, Luke and John are four 'takes' on Jesus. Their authors clearly believed that they were *good* takes, and that they show us Jesus as he really was. From what we've seen so far, we've got every reason to think this would be true. But the question is: *can we check?* Is there any way we can work out whether the Gospels really are good takes on Jesus?

PART 3

WHAT EVIDENCE IS THERE?

We've seen a number of good reasons to expect that the Gospels will give us an accurate picture of the real Jesus. But can we go beyond this expectation? Is there any way to check whether the Gospel writers succeeded in their goal of giving us an accurate picture of the real Jesus? There is, in fact, good evidence for the historical reliability of the Gospels. There is evidence from outside the Gospels (external evidence), and there is evidence within the Gospels themselves (internal evidence).[5]

External evidence

Virtually no serious scholar believes that Jesus didn't exist. This is partly because of external evidence—that is, information about Jesus that comes from *outside* the Gospels. This evidence comes from other ancient literature and from the findings of archaeology. Most importantly, there are several non-Christian sources that give us some fascinating information. These fall into two groups: references to Jesus from Greco-Roman sources and references from Jewish sources. For the sake of completeness, all the significant references are listed below.[6]

A. Greco-Roman references to Jesus

There are several references to Jesus in writings from the ancient world in which Christianity grew up. Here are seven pieces of evidence in this category:

i.   Julius Africanus, a third-century writer, refers in his work *History of the World* to a first-century Greek historian named Thallus who, he says, discusses the darkness that occurred at the time of Jesus' crucifixion (see Mark chapter 15, verse 33).

ii. Shortly after the fall of Jerusalem in AD 70, a man named Mara bar Serapion, in a letter to his son, refers to the Jews executing their "wise king". Most scholars regard this as a reference to Jesus, although it is far from clear.

iii. Pliny the Younger, a Roman governor in Bithynia, wrote early in the second century AD that Christians met regularly and sang hymns to Christ "as if to a god" (*Letters* 10.96.7).[7]

iv. At a similar time, the Roman historian Tacitus mentions that "Christ … had undergone the death penalty in the reign of Tiberius, by sentence of the procurator Pontius Pilate" (*Annals* 15.44).[8]

v. Around AD 120, Suetonius, another historian and friend of Pliny the Younger, speaks of a riot between Christians and Jews that broke out in Rome because of someone named "Chrestus" (*Life of Claudius* 25.4). This is probably a confused reference to Christ as the founder of Christianity.

vi. Lucian of Samosata (AD 115-200), a famous Greek writer, speaks of "the one whom [Christians] still worship, the man who was crucified in Palestine …" (*Death of Peregrinus* 11).[9]

vii. Around AD 175, another Greek writer called Celsus says that Jesus' mother had an affair with a Roman soldier, and that Jesus' miracles were actually Egyptian magic.

These references are mostly brief and sometimes questionable; but they are still important. At the very least, they tell us that Jesus lived in Palestine and was executed under Pontius Pilate (which all the Gospels record); that strange things were said to have happened at the time of Jesus' crucifixion; that people needed to offer alternative explanations for Jesus' birth and his miracles; and that Christians continued to worship Jesus after his death.

B. Non-Christian Jewish references to Jesus

Many of the early Christians, including the Gospel writers, were Jewish. There are also references to Jesus in non-Christian Jewish writings, which are not nearly as positive as the Gospels. There are four important references to Jesus by Jews who were not Christians:

i. In his great work *Jewish Antiquities*, first-century Jewish historian Josephus gives a fascinating description of Jesus and his treatment by Pontius Pilate. Most scholars think that Josephus didn't write all of this passage, and that some bits were probably added in later (these dubious bits are in square brackets below). But many of the more straightforward statements of this passage fit Josephus' style and are probably genuine. Here is what Josephus says:

> Now, there was about this time Jesus, a wise man, [if it be lawful to call him a man], for he was a doer of surprising deeds—a teacher of such men as receive the truth with pleasure. He drew over to him both many of the Jews, and many of the gentiles. [He was the Christ;] and when Pilate, at the suggestion of the principal men amongst us, had condemned him to the cross, those that loved him at the first did not forsake him, [for he appeared to them alive again the third day, as the divine prophets had foretold these and ten thousand other wonderful things concerning him;] and the tribe of Christians, so named from him, are not extinct to this day. (*Antiquities* 18.63-64)[10]

ii. Elsewhere, Josephus mentions both John the Baptist (*Antiquities* 18.116-119) and James, the brother of Jesus (*Antiquities* 20.200). In the later passage, James is described as "the brother of Jesus, who is called Christ".[11]

iii. A section of the Talmud (a compendium of rabbinic teaching) that dates from between AD 100 and AD 200 says that someone called Jesus was "hanged" (on a cross?) on the eve of Passover, and that he "practiced sorcery and led Israel astray" (*b. Sanhedrin* 43a-b).[12]

iv. A later section of the Talmud (probably written after AD 200)

claims, like Celsus (see above), that Jesus was the illegitimate son of a Roman soldier (*b. Shabbat* 104b). Most historians regard this as a later attempt to discredit the Christian beliefs about Jesus' birth.[13]

Again, these references are fairly brief and, in some places, uncertain. But they do provide support for several basic details: Jesus had a brother called James, who became an important leader in the early church; Jesus was crucified; John the Baptist was executed under Herod; and Jesus was a teacher who did things that could be described as "surprising deeds" and "sorcery".

C. Archaeological and geographical evidence

At a few points, archaeology also provides evidence for the reliability of the Gospels. For example, in 1888 the site of the pool of Bethesda (which is mentioned in John chapter 5, verse 2) was found, and excavations showed that it had five porticoes, which matches what John's Gospel says. We can also confirm that many of the geographical details mentioned in the Gospels are accurate. Many reports of Jesus' movements in the Gospels seem to be based on an accurate knowledge of the geography of Palestine, rather than a retrospective and fuzzy knowledge projected back by later Christian writers.

Internal evidence

Probably more significant than these external pieces of evidence, however, is evidence for reliability within the Gospels themselves. When the Gospels are examined and compared, we find a number of things to suggest that they're reliable historical documents.

A. Agreement

First, *the Gospels agree in many important respects*. When the Gospels are compared it is easy to notice the differences between them. These differences are important, and should not be ignored (see below); but they also shouldn't cause us to miss the remarkable agreement between the Gospels. Although they differ on what they include, and on what parts of Jesus' life they highlight, the four Gospels tell basically the same story about Jesus and have many things in common. All four Gospels agree that Jesus' public ministry was linked to John the Baptist's ministry, and that Jesus was baptized by John. All the Gospels agree that Jesus called a group of followers around himself. All the Gospels agree that Jesus had a public ministry in Galilee. All the Gospels agree that Jesus did remarkable healings. All the Gospels tell the story of Jesus miraculously feeding five thousand people.

All the Gospels report similar accusations against Jesus (e.g. that he was demon-possessed). All the Gospels are clear that Jesus was a teacher. All the Gospels record Jesus predicting that he would be betrayed. All the Gospels agree that shortly before he died Jesus caused a stir by riding into Jerusalem on a donkey, and that his actions in Jerusalem following this led to his arrest and execution. All the Gospels agree that Jesus came into conflict with the religious leaders of his day. All the Gospels record Jesus' prediction that Peter would deny him. And, most significantly, all the Gospels agree that Jesus was arrested at night in the Garden of Gethsemane, that he was tried before the Sanhedrin and then before the Roman Governor Pontius Pilate, that a bandit named Barabbas was pardoned instead of him, that Pilate ordered his execution, that he was crucified outside Jerusalem, that he died, that a number of women he had known witnessed his death, that he was buried in the tomb of Joseph of Arimathea, that the women went to the tomb on the following Sunday and found it empty, and that the explanation for this empty tomb was that he had been raised from the dead. The agreement on the basic details of Jesus' life is substantial and should give us confidence that the Gospels are reliable historical records.

B. Reasonable disagreement

Nevertheless, the Gospels do appear to disagree at some points. Many of these differences are very minor, but there are some that look to be more significant. Upon closer examination many of these differences can be adequately explained, although it's not always possible to prove beyond doubt that these explanations are correct. A few examples should illustrate the point:

i. *Sometimes small details appear to contradict one another.* As was mentioned before, Matthew and Mark record Jesus healing a different number of blind men on the Jericho Road. Similarly, Mark's Gospel records Jesus saying that the cock will not crow twice before Peter has denied Jesus three times (Mark chapter 14, verse 30), while the other Gospels record Jesus speaking only of the cock crowing (Matthew chapter 26, verse 34; Luke chapter 22, verse 34; John chapter 13, verse 38). This may, however, be explained by the fact that the second cock crow, at about 1:30am, was the most important. Whatever the case, we should note the substantial agreement: Jesus, Peter, betrayal, and the cock crowing!

ii. At some points, *one Gospel's version of a story appears to contradict another's.* For instance, in his account of a rich young man who came and spoke to Jesus, Mark records Jesus as saying, "Why do you call me good? No one is good except God alone" (Mark chapter 10, verse 18). But in his account of this event Matthew phrases this as, "Why do you ask me about what is good? There is only one who is good" (Matthew chapter 19, verse 17). This difference, however, may be because Matthew is simply re-phrasing Jesus' words to avoid potential misunderstanding in Mark's version. Apparent differences can often be resolved when we pay attention to the emphasis and message an author is trying to bring out.

iii. *Various sayings of Jesus are found in different contexts in different Gospels*. For example, parts of a long speech that Jesus makes from the Mount of Olives in Matthew's Gospel (Matthew chapters 24-25) are found in different situations in Luke's Gospel (compare Matthew chapter 24, verses 45-51 with Luke chapter 12, verses 41-48; and Matthew chapter 25, verses 14-30 with Luke chapter 19, verses 11-27). This, however, may be explained either by the common practice of rearranging speeches, or by the fact that Jesus probably said similar things on different occasions. It is also important to note that our obsession with chronology was not necessarily shared by all in the ancient world. Which brings us to the next point.

iv. *Matthew, Mark and Luke have a dramatically different chronology to that of John*. In them, Jesus appears to go to Jerusalem for the first time in the week before his death; but in John, Jesus goes to Jerusalem a number of times throughout his ministry. Again, however, it must be noted that Matthew, Mark and Luke do not rule out John's version of events. Just because they do not report earlier visits to Jerusalem, it doesn't mean they did not happen. As was mentioned above, the Gospels don't try to say everything, but instead are carefully constructed stories that include only selected information about Jesus' life.

v. *The resurrection accounts appear to contradict each other at a number of points*. For example:
   • The accounts report a different number of women going to Jesus' tomb: Luke says there were at least five, Mark says there were three, Matthew says there were two, and John records only one (Luke chapter 24, verse 10; Mark chapter 16, verse 1; Matthew chapter 28, verse 1; John chapter 20, verse 1).
   • Luke and John record the women encountering two mess-

engers in the tomb, but Matthew and Mark mention only one (Luke chapter 24, verse 4; John chapter 20, verse 12; Matthew chapter 28, verse 2; Mark chapter 16, verse 5).

- The accounts differ regarding what happened to the stone sealing the tomb (Matthew chapter 28, verse 2; Mark chapter 16, verse 4; Luke chapter 24, verse 2; John chapter 20, verse 1).
- The accounts record different appearances of Jesus to the disciples (compare Matthew chapter 28, verses 16-20 and Luke chapter 24, verses 36-53).

However, even at this point it can be shown that the accounts are not in fact contradictory (John Wenham has argued this point convincingly in his book *Easter Enigma*),[14] and that many of the apparent contradictions melt away on closer inspection. And, most importantly, as historian NT Wright comments, "… when placed side by side, [the Gospels] tell a tale which, despite the multiple surface inconsistencies, succeeds in hanging together. To put it crudely, the fact that they cannot agree over how many women, or angels, were at the tomb, or even the location of the appearances, does not mean that nothing happened."[15]

This is not to say that all the differences between the Gospels can be straightforwardly resolved, nor that there is nothing that requires further investigation. But it is to say that the apparent disagreements between them don't call their basic reliability into question. Indeed, if all four Gospels told the story exactly the same way, we might start to wonder if it was a bit too neat and tidy! On the other hand, if the Gospels told a fundamentally different story to each other, or if they could be shown at particular points to be clearly unreliable, then we would have a problem. But that is not what we find. When the specific difficulties are looked at carefully, possible explanations tend to appear.

C. The evidence of embarrassment

A final important piece of evidence is that there are features of the Gospel stories that would have been somewhat embarrassing when they were written, but which were nonetheless included. The most important example is that all the Gospels record how women found the tomb empty on the morning of the resurrection. This is important because in the first century, women were not generally accepted as legal witnesses. Their testimony was seen as unreliable. So this is not the kind of detail someone would invent. It's unlikely, to say the least, that Mark would have invented a story about the empty tomb and placed at its centre people whose testimony would be seen as unreliable. The temptation to remove this detail would have been great; and yet it remains. This strongly suggests that the Gospel authors were committed to telling the story as it happened.

Conclusion

From all this we can conclude a number of things. First, there is enough external evidence for us to conclude that Jesus was a real historical figure; the Gospel writers did not invent him. Second, where we can check the Gospels with external sources, they are reliable. Third, when the Gospels are examined carefully, they give us good reasons to think they are historically reliable. Their stories aren't identical in every detail—different things are emphasized, and different events are highlighted—but the broad picture remains clear, and there is substantial agreement on the important details. The Gospels show exactly the kinds of features we should expect from different accounts of the same events. There is every reason to think that their authors have followed through on their intentions to tell the truth about Jesus.

CONCLUSION

THE TRUSTWORTHINESS OF THE GOSPELS

I have argued that there are solid grounds for regarding the Gospels as historically reliable. They were written by people who were deeply concerned about speaking truthfully, who were committed to recounting history faithfully because they believed that was how God worked in the world, and who wanted people to know the truth about Jesus. This means we should expect to find the Gospels to be generally historically accurate. And this is what we do find. Aspects of the Gospels are supported by external sources, and they stand up to criticism when they are inspected carefully and compared with one another.

None of this should be a surprise. The early church cared deeply about the person and life of Jesus. As Paul wrote to the Corinthians:

> For I delivered to you as of first importance what I also received: that Christ died for our sins in accordance with the Scriptures, that he was buried, that he was raised on the third day in accordance with the Scriptures, and that he appeared to Cephas, then to the twelve. Then he appeared to more than five hundred brothers at one time, most of whom are still alive, though some have fallen asleep. Then he appeared to James, then to all the apostles. Last of all, as to one untimely born, he appeared also to me. (1 Corinthians chapter 15, verses 3-8)

It mattered to Paul that *Jesus had died*, and that *he had been buried*, and that *he had been raised on the third day*. And it mattered to Paul that Jesus had appeared alive, so he had his evidence ready! His readers could even go and ask some of the people who had seen the risen Jesus. The Christian faith is anchored in history, and if the things

that were said about Jesus didn't really happen, then Christianity is a joke. From very early on, the Christian church believed that people could trust what Matthew, Mark, Luke and John said about Jesus. For many solid, historical reasons, we can be confident that this opinion is still the right one.

And this, of course, is an exciting conclusion, because it means that you and I, 2000 years later, can read the Gospels and genuinely know the truth about Jesus. This is a truth worth exploring, because the real, historical Jesus isn't just a character of interest for academics. His actions and words have changed the lives of millions of people down through the ages. You'd be mad not to take up the chance to discover him for yourself.

APPENDIX

OTHER TAKES ON JESUS

But what about the 'other gospels'? The suggestion is frequently made that there are other gospels that show us the 'real' Jesus. The Gospels we have in our Bibles, it is said, are the product of later church tradition. Books like Dan Brown's *The Da Vinci Code* claim that the real Jesus is to be found in other sources. For the reasons outlined in this booklet, it is very unlikely that this way of looking at Matthew, Mark, Luke and John is in any way accurate. But what about these other sources? What do we know about them?

There is a lot of hot air spoken about the 'other gospels'. When people talk about other gospels, they are mostly talking about a number of works that were found in 1945 at a place in Egypt called Nag Hammadi. This discovery brought to light a large number of texts that had, until then, been known only in part, or through references from early Christian authors. Examples include the Gospel of Thomas, the Gospel of Philip and the Gospel of Mary. These last two are discussed in *The Da Vinci Code*. It is worth saying from the outset that almost no serious scholar regards the gospels of Philip and Mary as giving better access to the historical Jesus than the biblical Gospels. Both of these works were written much later than Matthew, Mark, Luke and John. The Gospel of Philip was probably written between the later part of the second century and the second half of the third century, and the Gospel of Mary was probably written towards the end of the second century. Both works give clear evidence of being composed under the influence of the philosophical ideas of this later period. To put it bluntly: they are Gnostic religious writings (Gnosticism was a philosophical/religious movement that was very widespread and influential in the second and third centuries).

Their authors have clearly taken on Christian ideas and thinking and adapted them to their own religious framework. They are interesting in their own way, but there is very little reason to view them as giving us any reliable information about Jesus. Similar things are true of the recently published Gospel of Judas. This, too, is a second-century Gnostic text with no real claim to historical accuracy.

The only work that some historians regard as potentially giving us access to the historical Jesus is the Gospel of Thomas. Arguments about this work are quite complicated; however, we should note some broad points. Firstly, Thomas is not a 'gospel' in any meaningful sense. It is, in fact, a collection of 114 sayings ascribed to Jesus. Some of these sayings are similar to sayings in Matthew, Mark, Luke and John (e.g. "Many who are first will become last"; Thomas 04:2);[16] others, such as the final saying, "Every woman who makes herself male will enter the kingdom of heaven" (Thomas 114:3), are not. The most likely explanation for the similar, or parallel, sayings is, in fact, that Thomas is dependent on the biblical Gospels, and that its author took various bits of Matthew, Mark and Luke, and changed them to reflect his own philosophy.

However, a bigger problem for those who regard Thomas as being dated very early has to do with the shape of the work as a whole. The early church, as we have seen, was born in a Jewish context with a Jewish background. This background was founded on belief in the God of the Old Testament, who acted within history. Matthew, Mark, Luke and John make sense in this context. They are stories anchored in the history of the first century and concerned to tell the truth about Jesus. Thomas, however, does not make sense in this context. Thomas is not concerned with Jesus' acts, but solely with his speech. In Thomas, Jesus is simply a teacher; he is not Israel's Messiah, bringing in the kingdom of God through his acts. Thomas thus makes much more sense as the product of later philosophical ideas than as the product of early Christianity.

ENDNOTES

1   It was either AD 30 or AD 33. For a couple of reasons AD 30 seems too early, so many scholars think Jesus was executed in AD 33.

2   The game is also called 'telephone', 'grapevine' and 'pass it down'. It involves children sitting in a line and passing a message by first hearing it whispered to them by the previous person in the line, and then whispering it to the next person in the line.

3   For more detail on this important point, see the excellent book by Richard Bauckham, *Jesus and the Eyewitnesses* (Grand Rapids, Eerdmans, 2008).

4   One reason for this is that the Gospel writers only had so much space to work with. In the first century, a standard book was written on a roll of papyrus. These rolls were normally 20-25cm high and up to about 9m long. The text of the book was written in lots of thin columns, 5-10cm wide, with 25-45 lines per column. This fixed size acted like a very firm word-limit (you couldn't just add a few pages and hope nobody noticed). So instead of just putting everything they knew down on paper, the Gospel writers had to make decisions about what their histories would look like—what they'd leave in and what they'd cut out.

5   For more detail on this question, see Craig Blomberg, 'Gospels (Historical Reliability)', *Dictionary of Jesus and the Gospels*, 1992, pp. 291-97.

6   For more detailed information about these references, see chapters 2 and 3 of John Dickson's excellent book *The Christ Files* (Blue Bottle, Sydney, 2006), on which this list is largely based.

7   Translation taken from *Pliny: Letters and Panegyricus*, vol. 2, trans. B Radice, Loeb Classical Library 59, Harvard University Press, Cambridge, 1969, p. 289.

8 Translation taken from *Tacitus: The Annals*, vol. 5, trans. J Jackson, Loeb Classical Library 322, Harvard University Press, Cambridge, 1991, p. 283.

9 Translation taken from *Lucian*, vol. 5, trans. AM Harmon, Loeb Classical Library 302, Harvard University Press, Cambridge, 1972, p. 13.

10 Translation taken from *Josephus: The Complete Works*, trans. W Whiston, Thomas Nelson, Nashville, 1998, p. 576.

11 ibid., pp. 581, 645.

12 Translation taken from J Schachter and H Freedman (trans), *The Babylonian Talmud: Seder Nezikin*, ed. I Epstein, vol. 3, Soncino, London, 1935, p. 281.

13 Translation taken from H Freedman (trans.), *The Babylonian Talmud: Seder Mo'ed*, ed. I Epstein, vol. 1, Soncino, London, 1938, p. 504.

14 J Wenham, *Easter Enigma*, illustrated edn, Wipf and Stock, Eugene, 2005.

15 NT Wright, *The Resurrection of the Son of God*, Christian Origins and the Question of God, vol. 3, SPCK, London, 2003, p. 614.

16 Quotations are from *The Gospel of Thomas*, tr. SJ Patterson and JM Robinson, in The Nag Hammadi Library, viewed 2 Feb 2009: www.gnosis.org/naghamm/gth_pat_rob.htm

FURTHER READING

Paul Barnett, *Is the New Testament History?*, rev. edn, Aquila Press, Sydney, 2003.

Richard Bauckham, *Jesus and the Eyewitnesses: The Gospels as Eyewitness Testimony*, Eerdmans, Grand Rapids, 2008.

Craig Blomberg, 'Gospels (Historical Reliability)', *Dictionary of Jesus and the Gospels*, 1992, pp. 291-97.

Craig Blomberg, *The Historical Reliability of the Gospels*, 2nd edn, IVP, Leicester, 2008.

John Dickson, *The Christ Files: How Historians Know What they Know About Jesus*, Blue Bottle Books, Sydney, 2006.

John Wenham, *Christ and the Bible*, 3rd edn, Eagle, Guildford, 1993.

John Wenham, *Easter Enigma*, illustrated edn, Wipf and Stock, Eugene, 2005.

NT Wright, *The Resurrection of the Son of God*, Christian Origins and the Question of God, vol. 3, SPCK, London, 2003.

NT Wright, *Jesus and the Victory of God*, Christian Origins and the Question of God, vol. 2, SPCK, London, 1996.

Matthias Media is an independent Christian publishing company based in Sydney, Australia. To browse our online catalogue, access samples and free downloads, and find more information about our resources, visit our website:

www.matthiasmedia.com.au

How to buy our resources

1. Direct from us over the internet:
   – in the US: www.matthiasmedia.com
   – in Australia and the rest of the world: www.matthiasmedia.com.au

2. Direct from us by phone:
   – in the US: 1 866 407 4530
   – in Australia: 1800 814 360 (Sydney: 9663 1478)
   – international: +61-2-9663-1478

3. Through a range of outlets in various parts of the world.
   Visit **www.matthiasmedia.com.au/international.php** for details about recommended retailers in your part of the world, including www.thegoodbook.co.uk in the United Kingdom.

4. Trade enquiries can be addressed to:
   – in the US and Canada: sales@matthiasmedia.com
   – in Australia and the rest of the world: sales@matthiasmedia.com.au